AGAINST THE ODDS

Nelson Mandela

Cath Senker

a Capstone company — publishers for children

Raintree is an imprint of Capstone Global Library Limited, a company incorporated in England and Wales having its registered office at 7 Pilgrim Street, London EC4V 6LB – Registered company number: 6695582

www.raintreepublishers.co.uk
myorders@raintreepublishers.co.uk

Edited by Linda Staniford and Jennifer Besel
Designed by Philippa Jenkins and Tim Bond
Picture research by Tracy Cummins
Production by Helen McCreath
Originated by Capstone Global Library Limited
Printed and bound in China by LEO

ISBN 978 1 406 29753 9
19 18 17 16 15
10 9 8 7 6 5 4 3 2 1

British Library Cataloguing in Publication Data
A full catalogue record for this book is available from the British Library.

Acknowledgements
We would like to thank the following for permission to reproduce photographs: Baileys Archives: Drum Photographer, 19; Corbis: Bernard Bisson, 29, Bettmann, 15, Hulton-Deutsch Collection, 11, Patrick Durand/Sygma, 27, 35, Peter Turnley, 36; Getty Images: ALEXANDER JOE/AFP, 34, API/Gamma-Rapho, 5, Bongani Mnguni/City Press/Gallo Images, 24, Clive Limpkin/Express, 30, Evans, 13, Hart Preston/The LIFE Picture Collection, 9, Hoberman Collection, 23, Jurgen Schadeberg, 10, 26, Keystone-France/Gamma-Keystone, 7, 17, Media24/Gallo Images, 43, Oryx Media Archive/Gallo Images, 38, Per-Anders Pettersson, 6, Rolls Press/Popperfoto, 12, Tom Stoddart, 32, Universal History Archive/UIG, 18, WALTER DHLADHLA/AFP, Cover, 31, William F. Campbell/The LIFE Picture Collection, 37; Granger NYC: ullstein bild, 14; Landov: PETER ANDREWS/Reuters, 40; Magnum Photos: Stuart Franklin, 21; Newscom: David Turnley/Corbis/Splash News, 33; Thinkstock: Micky Wiswedel, 41.

We would like to thank the following for permission to reproduce quoted text:
p23 Reproduced by kind permission of The Observer newspaper who published "The Guard who really was Mandela's friend" article, 20 May 2007; Reproduced by kind permission of A P Watt at United Agents on behalf of the Executors of the Estate of Nadine Gordimer; p33 ©Nelson Mandela, courtesy of Nelson Mandela Foundation; p43 taken from the book "Mandela: The Authorised Biography" by Anthony Sampson (Harper Press, HarperCollins UK, 1999).

Every effort has been made to contact copyright holders of material reproduced in this book. Any omissions will be rectified in subsequent printings if notice is given to the publisher.

All the internet addresses (URLs) given in this book were valid at the time of going to press. However, due to the dynamic nature of the internet, some addresses may have changed, or sites may have changed or ceased to exist since publication. While the author and publisher regret any inconvenience this may cause readers, no responsibility for any such changes can be accepted by either the author or the publisher.

Contents

Who was Nelson Mandela? 4

What was Nelson Mandela's
upbringing like? 6

How did Nelson Mandela get
into politics? 10

How did Nelson Mandela campaign
against apartheid? 14

How did Nelson Mandela lead
the ANC from prison? 22

How did the anti-apartheid movement
force change? 26

How did Nelson Mandela help
to end apartheid? 34

Continuing Nelson Mandela's work 42

Timeline 44

Glossary 45

Find out more 47

Index 48

Some words are shown in bold, **like this**. You can find out what
they mean by looking in the glossary.

Who was Nelson Mandela?

On 10 May 1994, a dignified man in his seventies, smartly dressed in a black suit, stood before a gathering of important people from 140 countries in the Union Buildings in Pretoria, capital city of South Africa. He solemnly accepted the office of **President** of South Africa and promised to devote himself to the well-being of his country, working towards peace between the different races that had fought each other for decades.

In the streets outside the Union Buildings, the atmosphere was electric. When the new president appeared, a crowd of 100,000 black and white South Africans cheered wildly, singing and dancing in celebration.

Against the odds, Nelson Mandela had just been elected as the country's first black president. The eyes of the whole world were on this significant event.

ANC leader

From 1948, white people ruled the mostly black country of South Africa. Nelson Mandela became a leader of the African National Congress (ANC), which fought for **democracy**. He was sent to prison, but remained an important figure. After 27 years he was finally released, and within four years, he became president.

UNDER EUROPEAN CONTROL

From the 19th century, European countries ruled most African lands. Britain governed South Africa until 1910, when white **settlers** took power. In the 20th century, movements for **independence** grew in all African countries. By 1980, they had all gained independence from white rule – except South Africa.

This is Nelson Mandela as a young man in 1950, at the start of his fight against **apartheid**.

What was Nelson Mandela's upbringing like?

Nelson Mandela was born in 1918 in the Transkei, a coastal area of South Africa. He was the son of Chief Henry Mandela of the Madiba clan (family group). His mother became a **Methodist** Christian, giving up her traditional African religious customs. Nelson grew up in the countryside, playing in the hills, swimming in freshwater pools and eating freshly roasted corn on the cob. But when he was just nine, his father died, and the Regent (acting ruler) Jongintaba of the Thembu people took Nelson in.

This is the village of Qunu, where Nelson grew up. He used to play in the hills above the village.

Miners in the Robinson mine near Johannesburg, 1900, hacked through rock by hand to search for gold.

Regent Jongintaba ruled his community but had little power. In 1910, white settlers had formed the Union of South Africa and taken over most of the land. Under the 1913 Natives' Land Act, they set aside just 7 per cent of the land for the African people, who made up four-fifths of the population. Black people were at the bottom of society, working as labourers on white people's farms or in the mines, doing the dirty, dangerous, low-paid jobs. The government did not allow them to vote.

RACiSM

European people settled in South Africa from the 17th century. Mostly Dutch, German or French, they became known as Boers and later **Afrikaners**. British settlers arrived from the 19th century. With their deadly weapons, they fought to take the land from Africans. Europeans held views that would be considered **racist** today. They felt it was right for white people to control the country and its resources.

Schoolboy and student

Jongintaba was a Methodist, and he gave young Nelson a Christian education. From the age of 16, Nelson attended Methodist boarding schools, where he studied British history and geography.

Despite his British education, Nelson believed in **Ubuntu**, the African idea that people were human beings because they were part of a community. Even as a teenager, he always saw the best in others.

Expelled for his principles

After finishing school in 1938, Nelson attended South African Native College (later the University College of Fort Hare). However, he was **expelled** for campaigning against the terrible food served to the African students. He decided it was more important to stick up for his community than to complete his course.

"White university students looked down on black students and shunned them. When Nelson sat down in the university library, a white student moved away. But Nelson never bore grudges. When he became president, he invited his university companions to a get-together, remarking, 'I am what I am both as a result of people who respected and helped me, and of those who did not respect me and treated me badly.' "

Based on Anthony Sampson's biography of Nelson Mandela

However, Nelson still wanted to become a lawyer and from 1943 to 1948 he studied law at the University of Witwatersrand, Johannesburg. Later, he passed an exam that allowed him to act as a lawyer. At the time, very few black South Africans became lawyers.

This is Witwatersrand University in 1943, where black and white students studied together; however, only 5–6 per cent of students were black.

How did Nelson Mandela get into politics?

Living in the large, busy city of Johannesburg, Mandela became involved in politics. He joined the ANC and in 1944 became the leader of its new Youth League. It was the start of a struggle for black freedom that would last his whole life. In the same year, Mandela met and married Evelyn Ntoto Mase, and soon their son, Thembi, was born.

Nelson Mandela and fellow ANC **activist** Ruth First attended an ANC conference in 1951.

Programme of action

During the 1940s, many black people headed to the big cities to look for work in industry and business. The ANC Youth League aimed to attract these workers to the movement for black rights. It drew up a programme of action against the racist government, calling for strikes, protests and **boycotts** (refusing to buy goods or use services).

Mandela and his companions borrowed ideas from the independence movement in India. There, Mahatma Gandhi led a campaign of non-violent protest against British rule. Gandhi believed that if most people simply refused to follow the rules, it would become impossible to govern the country. In India, this plan succeeded and the country won independence in 1947.

Who's who

The African National Congress

African leaders set up the South African Native National Congress in 1912 to fight against the loss of their rights. It was renamed the African National Congress in 1923 and became the main African protest organization in South Africa. The ANC argued that Africans should have the same rights as Europeans, including the right to vote.

In 1930, Mahatma Gandhi walked in a civil disobedience march in India to protest against British rule.

Mahatma Gandhi

Apartheid – separating the races

If the ANC thought the situation was bad in the 1940s, it was about to grow worse. In 1948, the Afrikaner-run National Party took power and brought in apartheid – racial separation. The racist attitudes that had developed since Europeans arrived became the law of the land.

A divided people

Apartheid changed everyone's lives. People were divided into four racial groups, and each group had to live in its own area, go to its own schools and use separate buses, hospitals, parks and beaches.

Under apartheid, black and white people had to use separate services, including taxis.

These are Asian schoolteachers in Durban in 1955; Asian children attended their own separate schools.

It was illegal to marry someone of another race, so mixed families were split up and family members forced to live in different areas. The best places were reserved for white people; Asians and "**Coloured**" (mixed-race) people lived in poorer parts.

RACE LAWS

The Population Registration Act of 1950 divided people into white, Asian, Coloured and Bantu (black). To count as white, a person had to look white and have parents classed as white. Any African was Bantu, while those with a white and a black parent were called Coloured. Most Asians came from India.

Black people (Bantu) were supposed to live in their **Bantustan**, the place where they were born. So Mandela should have returned to the Transkei. But like many other black South Africans, he remained in the city. The Bantustans were the poorest areas with the fewest natural resources and worst facilities. To enter white areas to work, black people had to show a pass book – like a passport for going to another country. The ANC now had an even harder job to fight for equal rights.

How did Nelson Mandela campaign against apartheid?

Mandela realized his legal training would be helpful in the fight against apartheid. In 1952, he and another black lawyer, Oliver Tambo, set up the first black South African law practice to help people who had broken the apartheid laws.

This picture shows Nelson Mandela and Oliver Tambo in 1960. Lots of ordinary black South Africans needed a defence lawyer in court after breaking one of the many apartheid laws.

The Defiance Campaign

In the same year, the ANC launched the Defiance Campaign to encourage black Africans to disobey the apartheid rules. Following Gandhi's tactic of non-violent protest, people burnt their pass books in public and stormed into whites-only areas of public places.

Lilian Ngoyi
(1911–1980)

Lilian Ngoyi joined the ANC during the Defiance Campaign and was arrested for entering the white area of a post office. She was a lively speaker, and was elected president of the ANC Women's League. In 1956, she led a women's march against the Pass Laws (see page 19) in Pretoria, one of the biggest anti-apartheid demonstrations in South Africa. Along with Mandela and other ANC leaders, she was arrested in December 1956 (see page 16).

Mandela travelled around the country to build support for the actions and got involved, too. He liked to be among the protesters, accepting the risks as they did. Thousands of campaigners were arrested, including Mandela. He was stopped for walking in a white part of Johannesburg at night.

Following the Defiance Campaign, Mandela and other leading activists received **banning orders**. Mandela wasn't allowed to leave Johannesburg, make speeches or attend meetings. The banning order was a huge obstacle to his activities but he managed to work around it. He developed a clever method of communicating secretly through a network of people without having to meet in public.

This group of protesters took over a "whites only" carriage on a train in Cape Town, in defiance of the apartheid laws, in 1952.

The Freedom Charter

In 1955, the ANC along with Indian and Coloured organizations bravely defied their banning orders to meet at the Congress of the People. Mandela strongly believed that everybody who opposed apartheid should work together.

More than 3,000 people attended. The Congress adopted the Freedom Charter, which Mandela had helped to write. It called for democracy in South Africa.

Who's who

Winnie Mandela
(born 1936)

Winnie and Nelson Mandela enjoyed just a short time together because Mandela was imprisoned in 1962. The government also punished Winnie for her ANC activity, with banning orders, **house arrest** and sometimes prison sentences. Yet she never stopped her ANC work. In 1988, people who worked with Winnie were accused of attacking four young men, which damaged her reputation.

Treason trial

Furious about the Congress, the government clamped down on the protest movement. In 1956, the police arrested 156 of the movement's leaders, including Mandela, and put them on trial for treason (betraying their country) and being **communists**. Mandela made important statements during the trial, defending their actions and showing he had become a leader of the movement.

The trial dragged on until 1961, when all the accused were proven not guilty and they were released. They had narrowly escaped life imprisonment or even the **death penalty**.

By this time, Nelson Mandela and his wife, Evelyn, had grown apart, partly because she was not involved in politics. Mandela divorced Evelyn and left his three children. In 1958, he married Winnie Madikizela, an enthusiastic ANC activist, and they had two daughters.

Nelson Mandela

This photo shows the 156 defendants
at the start of the Treason Trial.

Massacre at Sharpeville

In the late 1950s, the anti-apartheid movement held heated debates over what to do next. Mandela and the ANC argued for continuing to work with all races. But some activists were convinced that black people alone should fight for their freedom, and they left to form the Pan Africanist Congress (PAC) in 1959.

In 1960, both groups protested against the Pass Laws. At one demonstration in Sharpeville, a town in an area of South Africa known as Transvaal, fights broke out between the police and the protesters. The police panicked, opened fire and killed 69 protesters in a massacre that shocked the world. The government's response was to ban the ANC and PAC.

Protesters flee as fighting breaks out at the Sharpeville demonstration of 1960.

In December 1961, MK and another military group attacked this tower supporting electricity power lines in an act of sabotage.

Shift to sabotage

The Sharpeville massacre was a turning point. Mandela felt that non-violent protests were not working. He called for **sabotage** (destroying buildings or equipment) to make the country hard to govern and to force change. It was a tough decision to turn to **armed struggle**.

In 1961, the ANC set up a military group, Umkhonto we Sizwe (MK), to carry out sabotage attacks. MK bombed government buildings, railway stations and power lines.

To avoid arrest, Mandela had to go into hiding. He moved from place to place, sleeping in **"safe houses"** and never coming home.

PASSES

The Pass Law of 1952 forced black South Africans to carry an ID booklet that included their photo, place of birth, and work and criminal records. Anyone found without a pass could be arrested and sent to jail. It was impossible to travel freely.

Capture!

In 1962, Mandela began a tour of African countries to seek support for the ANC and train in sabotage methods. In July 1962, MK sent him an urgent message to return home. Once back, he occasionally appeared in public rather than remaining in hiding. The police quickly tracked down Mandela, arresting him and other ANC leaders.

A life sentence

At the Rivonia Trial of ANC leaders in 1963–4, Mandela declared that the law was unfair and so the protesters were right to resist it. Again, the odds were stacked against Mandela and he could have been sentenced to death. But in 1964, he and other leaders were instead sentenced to life imprisonment.

At the Rivonia Trial on 20 April 1964, Mandela stated:

"All lawful modes of expressing opposition to this principle [of white rule] had been closed by legislation [laws], and we were placed in a position in which we had either to accept a permanent state of inferiority [low position], or to defy [disobey] the government. We chose to defy the law."

Mandela and seven others were sent to Robben Island prison. The conditions in prison were terrible. Inmates had to do exhausting work, breaking stones in the hot sun, and the food was dreadful. Nelson Mandela faced the massive challenge of prison life. And how could he lead the struggle while behind bars?

Prisoners worked hard hammering stones at Robben Island prison. Mandela later told how they had to work fast or the warders would shout at them to speed up.

How did Nelson Mandela lead the ANC from prison?

Mandela had an extraordinary talent for befriending people and quickly became a leader inside prison. He spent time with the other imprisoned anti-apartheid activists, encouraging them to discuss the struggle for freedom and listen to each other's ideas.

Mandela also made friends with the prison warders (guards). Warders and prisoners alike came to him with their problems because they knew he would listen carefully and give good advice.

A prison "university"

Mandela stood up for the prisoners, complaining about problems and demanding better conditions. For example, from 1962 he was allowed to continue his law studies. He argued that all prisoners should have the right to study and this was granted in 1963. Some of his fellow inmates had entered prison unable to read, but they left with academic degrees.

Mandela developed his own ideas by reading the works of world leaders. He read books by Afrikaners to understand their way of thinking and he even learnt their language, Afrikaans.

"He was down-to-earth and courteous [polite]. He treated me with respect and my respect for him grew. After a while, even though he was a prisoner, a friendship grew... He wrote to my wife telling her that I must continue my studies. Even as a prisoner he was encouraging a warder to study."

Christo Brand, a young warder at Robben Island prison

This was Mandela's prison cell on Robben Island. The prison is now a museum about apartheid, with former prisoners as tour guides.

Secret contacts

It was tricky for Mandela to stay in touch with the world outside prison. He managed to smuggle letters to ANC leader Oliver Tambo by passing them to visiting lawyers or asking departing prisoners to hide them in their baggage.

School children in Soweto are seen protesting at the start of the uprising of June 1976. The revolt spread rapidly across the country.

Black Consciousness

Meanwhile, the Black Consciousness movement arose in the 1970s. It encouraged black people to be proud of their race and not to feel that whites were better than them. On 16 June 1976, thousands of children in Soweto, near Johannesburg, took to the streets in an **uprising** because they were angry about being forced to learn half of their lessons in Afrikaans. Although they were just children, the police opened fire and killed two protesters, including 12-year-old Hector Pieterson. Fighting continued into the night, and the death toll rose to at least 23.

News of this terrible event reached Mandela through new prisoners who arrived at Robben Island. Showing his continued involvement with the anti-apartheid movement, Mandela wrote a statement supporting the Soweto students. His words were smuggled out by prisoner Mac Maharaj when he was released that December.

Who's who

Steve Biko
(1946–1977)

Steve Biko was a leader of the Black Consciousness movement. In 1973, he was banned from teaching or going to meetings but he managed to organize reading, dressmaking and health education classes. In 1977, after the Soweto Uprising, the police arrested Biko. After several weeks of extremely brutal treatment, he died of his injuries. His funeral turned into a huge protest against the government.

How did the anti-apartheid movement force change?

From the late 1970s, the anti-apartheid movement grew and grew. White groups joined the campaign, including some church leaders, women's groups, students and writers.

One group was the Black Sash movement, an organization of mostly white women who opposed racial **discrimination**. They demonstrated against the unfairness of the Pass Laws. These women set up advice offices to help people affected by the Pass Laws and other apartheid rules.

Women of the Black Sash organization protested against the apartheid laws outside Johannesburg City Hall, around 1955.

Botha's reforms

Prime Minister P.W. Botha thought that bringing in a few reforms (improvements) might stop the wave of protest. In 1979, he allowed black people to form **trade unions**. The demonstrators saw reform as a sign that their protests were having an impact. Instead of stopping, they became even more determined to struggle to end apartheid.

Miners held a mass protest against poor safety standards after a fire in the Kinross gold mine, Eastern Transvaal, killed 177 miners in 1986.

The black trade unions used their power to hold protests and strikes in the mining industry. Mining was one of South Africa's most important industries, and the mainly black workforce could bring it to a halt. This put even more pressure on the government.

Who's who

Pieter Willem Botha
(1916–2006)

P.W. Botha was South Africa's prime minister from 1978 to 1984 and president from 1984 to 1989. In 1983, he brought in a new constitution (system of laws) that set up houses of parliament for Coloured people and Indians but left out black people because they were supposed to live in the Bantustans. It was a disaster. White people who supported apartheid were annoyed that non-whites were now involved in government, while anti-apartheid protesters were not satisfied.

The UDF – uniting against apartheid

By the 1980s, anti-apartheid campaigners were extremely frustrated at the lack of change. In 1983, more than 500 anti-apartheid groups came together to form the United Democratic Front (UDF). The UDF had one clear aim: to end apartheid. A message from Mandela, now in Pollsmoor prison, was read out and he was named as the UDF's patron (special supporter).

The white South African author Nadine Gordimer wrote about how apartheid damaged ordinary people's lives:

"People are shocked by police brutality when there's a funeral of some riot victim, but brutality doesn't just consist of killing people. There are other ways of hurting them, damaging them, that go on every day."

People power

The UDF organized a successful boycott of Botha's parliaments for Indian and Coloured people. It set up local committees that aimed to run townships (black towns), factories and schools through "people power". In some places, committees managed to run their community for a while, and people's courts replaced the law courts.

Botha's reforms had clearly failed, so he decided to crush the campaigners by force. In 1985, he declared a State of Emergency, banning anti-apartheid organizations and placing activists under house arrest. But people refused to stay at home and the number of protests increased.

In Cape Town, 1985, police used sticks to batter demonstrators protesting for the release of Nelson Mandela.

South Africa shunned

By now, the South African government was under intense pressure from the international community, too. By 1986, the United States, European countries and many others had introduced **economic sanctions**. This meant they stopped doing business with South Africa in protest against apartheid.

Many countries also boycotted South African sport, refusing to compete against South African teams because the country did not allow people of different races to play or watch sport together. Like a bully being shunned, South Africa was deliberately left out of the family of nations as a punishment for apartheid.

Anti-apartheid protesters in London marched outside the hotel where white South African cricketers were staying, in 1965. In 1970, the International Cricket Council banned South Africa from international cricket because of their anger at apartheid.

Winnie Mandela and her grandson, Ntsika, marked Nelson Mandela's 70th birthday in Johannesburg, 1988.

Free Nelson Mandela

During the 1980s, the Free Nelson Mandela campaign grew stronger. On Mandela's 70th birthday in 1988, anti-apartheid activists organized a concert in London that included global music stars Stevie Wonder, George Michael and Whitney Houston. It was broadcast to 67 other countries and boosted support for the movement.

A BANNED LEADER

Within South Africa, Nelson Mandela's words and teachings were banned. It was illegal to mention his name in the media or to show his picture. Student activists wore Nelson Mandela T-shirts and badges to defy the law, knowing that they could be arrested for doing so. In 1985, one teenage activist was sent to prison for 30 days for drinking from a mug with Mandela's face on it.

A country in chaos

By the late 1980s, South Africa was a country torn apart by divisions, including within the black community.

Bitter **rivalry** existed between the ANC and the Inkatha movement led by Mangosutho Buthelezi in the KwaZulu Bantustan. The Inkatha movement opposed the ANC's armed struggle and called for cooperation (working together) with the government. ANC and Inkatha supporters in the Transvaal and Natal frequently clashed. It was later proved that the government had armed Inkatha forces and encouraged them to fight the ANC to increase the divisions between black people.

This photo shows two young people running past a burning truck, which was set alight during a violent confrontation between ANC and Inkatha supporters in Tokosa township, Johannesburg, in 1994.

This man, suspected of betraying the ANC to the police, was almost "necklaced". He was saved by churchmen before the tyre was lit.

Black on black violence

Anti-apartheid activists also committed violence, attacking people they believed had betrayed the anti-apartheid movement to the police. One deadly method was "necklacing". This involved placing a petrol-filled tyre around a suspect's neck and setting it on fire. To try and stop this "black on black" violence, Mandela urged Buthelezi to work with the ANC but his pleas were ignored.

"In my entire political career few things have distressed me (so much) as to see our people killing one another as is now happening... It is a matter which requires the urgent attention of all people in this country. Nothing will please me more than to know that my concern and appeal have not fallen on deaf ears."

Part of a letter from Mandela to Buthelezi, written in 1989

How did Nelson Mandela help to end apartheid?

In the late 1980s, Mandela took the highly risky decision to negotiate (try to reach an agreement) with the government, even though he remained behind bars. Some senior ANC members disagreed with this approach, arguing that they needed to seize power by force, otherwise, they believed, white people would keep control.

However, Mandela met President Botha, and later President Frederik Willem de Klerk, and explained that as South Africa's black leader, he offered the only way out of the crisis in the country. Many senior people in government and society realized that they had to introduce democracy.

In 1990, de Klerk ended the ban on anti-apartheid organizations. Finally, after 27 years, Mandela was released from prison and was welcomed by joyful crowds.

Nelson and Winnie Mandela raised their fists in the ANC salute as Nelson Mandela walked free from jail on 11 February 1990.

This photo shows the extremist Afrikaner Resistance Movement marching in 1990. Its members wanted to keep apartheid and set up a separate state for Afrikaners.

Obstacles to peace

Next came the tricky part. Mandela, now president of the ANC, held long discussions with de Klerk's government about ending apartheid. There were huge obstacles: disagreements about how to run the country, continuing violence between the Inkatha Freedom Party (IFP, see box) and the ANC, and threats from **extremist** Afrikaners who did not accept change.

It seemed that South Africa could slip into civil war. But Mandela used his powerful negotiating skills and understanding of the Afrikaner people to steer the country peacefully towards democracy.

Who's who

Mangosutho Buthelezi
(born 1928)

Buthelezi became the chief minister of the KwaZulu Bantustan in 1976. He formed the Inkatha movement in 1975, in order to challenge the ANC. In 1990, he turned Inkatha into a political party, the IFP. It took part in the 1994 elections and Buthelezi entered Mandela's government as Minister of Home Affairs.

The first black president

South Africa changed rapidly during the early 1990s. All apartheid laws were scrapped, Mandela agreed to share power with the Afrikaners in a democratic South Africa and sanctions ended. In the country's first multi-racial elections in 1994, the ANC was the clear winner and Mandela made history by becoming the country's first black president.

Changing laws was the easy part. Now all adults, regardless of race, could vote and apply for government jobs. But changing the apartheid economy and society was far more challenging. Mandela introduced the Reconstruction and Development Programme, or RDP (1994–1999) in order to improve black living standards. It aimed to build schools and houses, provide electricity and clean water, and create new jobs in poor black communities.

Black South Africans queued patiently to vote for the very first time in the 1994 election.

These black students studied in an overcrowded class of more than 70 students at a school in Alexandria township near Johannesburg, 1990.

The black–white divide

Despite this programme, a huge divide remained between the rich, who were mostly white, and the poor, who were mainly black. Apartheid continued in daily life. White businesses usually employed white people and most people still mixed only with others of the same race. The country suffered from a high crime rate and the serious health problems of HIV/AIDS. Some argued Mandela should have done more to create a fairer society.

Failings of the Reconstruction and Development Programme (RDP)

Many people criticized the RDP. They were angry at how long it took to build new homes. People complained about the poor quality of the housing and the medical treatment in the clinics.

The Truth and Reconciliation Commission

Mandela had the difficult task of bringing together a divided society. How could the victims and **perpetrators** of apartheid (people who had carried out the policy) come to terms with what had happened?

Mandela set up the Truth and Reconciliation Commission (TRC) in 1995 to investigate the crimes of apartheid, using the idea of Ubuntu (see page 8). The aim was to heal relations between people.

ANC members gave evidence about apartheid crimes to the TRC. The ANC suffered from wrongdoing but was also found responsible for carrying out crimes against its enemies.

Desmond Tutu

(born 1931)

Desmond Tutu was a Christian priest and leader of the South African Council of Churches from 1978. He always spoke out against apartheid and supported non-violent protests. In 1995, Mandela made him head of the TRC. Tutu's job was to guide the commission. He had an extraordinary way of bringing people together and helping them to understand each other's point of view.

Speaking out

The TRC allowed victims and perpetrators to speak out about what had happened during apartheid so that they could understand each other. At public hearings (meetings in court), victims explained how loved ones had been beaten, tortured and murdered. Perpetrators confessed to their crimes so that victims knew what had happened to their family members. Some victims were able to forgive the crimes and some perpetrators managed to apologize.

However, critics of the TRC said it was too kind to the perpetrators. They avoided punishment, while victims waited a long time for **compensation**. Police officers revealed how they had killed anti-apartheid activists, but many people in government who were responsible for apartheid remained unpunished. Overall though, most people saw the Ubuntu method as helpful.

South Africa after Mandela

The 1990s brought major changes in Mandela's personal life. He and Winnie Mandela had grown apart, and in 1996, they divorced. Two years later, Mandela married Mozambican politician Graça Machel. Then in 1999, the elderly president handed over his job to Thabo Mbeki.

Mbeki tried to cope with the rising crime rate and the growing problem of HIV/AIDS. He also encouraged other countries to invest in Africa.

Thabo Mbeki became president of South Africa in 1999. He made great efforts to set up African organizations so that Africans could sort out their own problems.

Jacob Zuma

(born 1942)

Jacob Zuma was an ANC activist who spent 10 years in prison on Robben Island. After his release, he continued to work for the ANC. He became President of South Africa in 2009 after Mbeki resigned. Despite charges of corruption, Zuma remained popular in the ANC and was still President in 2014.

This photo shows Du Noon township, near Cape Town, in 2011. Many black South Africans still live in poor, cramped conditions in shacks like these.

Problems for the ANC

In 2005, Mbeki's deputy, Jacob Zuma, was charged with corruption (dishonest dealings), although the charges were later dropped. Some ANC members were unhappy with the party's policies, arguing that it was failing to improve the poor living conditions of many black people or create jobs. They broke away to set up the Congress of the People in 2008, promising that the new party would tackle crime, poverty and unemployment. However, the ANC remained in power. It won the general election in 2009 and Zuma became President.

Clearly, many problems remained in South Africa after apartheid. But Nelson Mandela had left a unified country with a working democracy, 20 years after his presidency.

Continuing Nelson Mandela's work

Mandela didn't stop working when he retired from politics. He continued to work with the Nelson Mandela Children's Fund, which he had founded in 1995 to help disabled children, orphans (children with no parents) and children with HIV/AIDS. Every year he invited children who'd been helped by the Fund to come to his birthday party.

He set up two new charities, including the Nelson Mandela Foundation. In 2009, it created Mandela Day, on 18 July – Mandela's birthday – to promote community service around the world. For example, on Mandela Day in 2013, in Grahamstown, Eastern Cape, student and community groups traded their skills or hobbies with others to help local people.

Nelson Mandela last appeared in public in 2010 and in 2013 he died, aged 95. For a week, South Africans of all races mourned their first black president.

"Mandela had learnt the hard way about the difficulties of reconciliation [restoring good relations], and he had seen how narrowly the country had avoided a bloodbath.... in jail he had seen how Afrikaners could be changed.... With all this personal experience he was uniquely able to establish a 'rainbow cabinet' which was one of the few genuinely multi-racial governments in the world."

Mandela's biographer, Anthony Sampson

Mandela's legacy

Mandela is remembered for his decades-long fight against apartheid. He decided when to end the armed struggle and played a key role in the complicated job of ending apartheid, sharing power with the Afrikaners who had imprisoned him. Against the odds, Mandela helped to achieve a multi-racial democracy in South Africa.

This photo shows Nelson Mandela on his 88th birthday. He achieved the ending of apartheid because he led a mass movement dedicated to the struggle for democracy.

Timeline

1918
Nelson Mandela is born on 18 July

1944
Mandela becomes leader of the ANC Youth League

1948
The National Party comes to power and introduces apartheid

1952
Mandela and Oliver Tambo set up the first black law practice in Johannesburg. The ANC launches the Defiance Campaign.

The Pass Law forces Africans to carry ID booklets

1955
The ANC and other anti-apartheid organizations attend the Congress of the People and adopt the Freedom Charter

1956
The police arrest 156 leaders of the Congress of the People and put them on trial

1959
The Pan Africanist Congress (PAC) forms

1960
At a demonstration in Sharpeville, Transvaal, the police kill 69 protesters

1961
The ANC sets up Umkhonto we Sizwe (MK)

1964
Mandela and other ANC leaders are sentenced to life imprisonment

1970s
The Black Consciousness movement arises

1976
Thousands of children in Soweto, near Johannesburg, take part in an uprising and two protesters are shot dead by police

1983
The United Democratic Front (UDF) is launched

Botha brings in a new constitution that sets up houses of parliament for "Coloured" people and Indians

1985
Botha declares a State of Emergency

1990
Nelson Mandela is released from prison

Mangosutho Buthelezi forms the Inkatha Freedom Party (IFP)

1994
The ANC wins the first multi-racial elections and Nelson Mandela becomes President of South Africa

1994–1999
The Reconstruction and Development Programme provides new homes, schools, electricity and running water to poor black areas

1995
The Truth and Reconciliation Commission (TRC) is set up to investigate apartheid crimes

1999
Mandela hands over the presidency to Thabo Mbeki

2013
Nelson Mandela dies, aged 95

Glossary

activist person who works to achieve political or social change

Afrikaner white South African whose family first came to South Africa from the Netherlands, Germany or France

apartheid political system in South Africa that divided people into four races: white, Coloured, Asian and black. Each race had to live and work separately. Only white people had full political rights.

armed struggle using violence for political aims, such as blowing up buildings

banning order order banning someone from activities in public, such as meeting other people or making speeches

Bantustan "homeland" for black people in South Africa

boycott refuse to buy, use or take part in something as a way of protesting

Coloured South African word used under apartheid for a person with one white and one black parent

communist person who supported the kind of government in the former Soviet Union, where the government was in charge of making goods and running services

compensation money given to someone because they have been hurt

death penalty punishment for a crime by execution (putting someone to death)

democracy political system in which all adults can vote for the rulers of the country

discrimination treating a particular group in society unfairly, for example, because of their race

economic sanction when a country stops economic links, such as trade, with another country because it is doing something bad

expel force to leave

extremist person with extreme views, for example, about politics. Extremist Afrikaners in the early 1990s did not accept the need to change the apartheid government.

house arrest when a person is kept prisoner in their home, rather than a prison

independence freedom from control by another country

Methodist member of the Methodist Church, an English Church that was brought to South Africa in the 19th century

perpetrator person who commits a crime or does something that is wrong

president after a change in the constitution in 1984, the head of government in South Africa

prime minister head of government in South Africa from 1910 to 1984, when the constitution changed and the president became the ruler

racist someone who believes that their race is better than others

rivalry when two people or groups compete. The African National Congress and the Inkatha Freedom Party competed for political power.

sabotage causing deliberate damage to buildings, equipment or transport systems (for example, railway stations) to protest about something

safe house secret house used by people who are in hiding from the police

settler person who goes to live in a new country or area

trade union organization of workers that acts to improve their working conditions

Ubuntu idea that people are not only individuals but live in a community and must share things and care for each other

uprising when people join together to fight the people in power

Find out more

Books

History Makers: Nelson Mandela, Sarah Ridley (Franklin Watts, 2013)

Long Walk to Freedom, Nelson Mandela, abridged by Chris van Wyk
(Macmillan Children's Books, 2010)

Nelson Mandela, Kadir Nelson (HarperCollins, 2013)

Nelson Mandela, Katie Daynes (Usborne, 2014)

The Children's Madiba: The Life Story of Nelson Mandela, Sean Fraser
(Penguin Global, 2014)

Websites

www.aamarchives.org
This website is all about the British anti-apartheid movement and includes
photos, videos and interviews, with videos of demonstrations and concerts.

www.anc.org.za/kids
This is a website about the ANC for younger readers.

www.bbc.co.uk/schools/primaryhistory/famouspeople/nelson_mandela
This BBC website provides a short biography of Nelson Mandela with lots of
photos and a quiz.

www.mandela-children.org.uk/nelson-mandela/242#
This website for the Nelson Mandela Children's Fund includes information
about Nelson Mandela's work for charity.

Index

African National Congress (ANC) 4, 10, 11, 13, 14, 16, 18, 19, 20, 24, 32, 33, 34, 35, 36, 38, 40, 41
Afrikaner Resistance Movement 35
Afrikaners 7, 12, 22, 35, 36, 43
anti-apartheid movement 5, 14–20, 25–31, 33, 34
apartheid 5, 12–13, 15, 27, 35, 37

banning orders 15, 16, 18, 25, 28
Bantustans 13, 27
Biko, Steve 25
Black Consciousness movement 25
Black Sash movement 26
Botha, P.W. 26, 27, 28, 34
boycotts 11, 28, 30
Buthelezi, Mangosutho 32, 33, 35

Coloured people 13, 27, 28
Congress of the People 41

de Klerk, F.W. 34
Defiance Campaign 14–15
democracy 4, 16, 34, 35, 41, 43

economic sanctions 30, 36

First, Ruth 10
Free Nelson Mandela campaign 31
Freedom Charter 16

Gandhi, Mahatma 11, 14

HIV/AIDS 37, 40, 42

Inkatha 32, 35
Inkatha Freedom Party (IFP) 35

Jongintaba, Regent 6, 7, 8

Machel, Graça 40
Madikizela-Mandela, Winnie 16, 31, 34, 40
Mandela, Nelson
    ANC member and leader 4, 10, 35
    children 10, 16
    death of 42
    early life 6
    education 8
    family background 6
    imprisonment 4, 16, 20–24, 25
    lawyer 9, 14
    marries Evelyn Mase 10
    marries Graça Machel 40
    marries Winnie Madikizela 16
    President of South Africa 4, 36
    released from prison 34
    Treason Trial 16, 17
Mandela Day 42
Mase, Evelyn 10, 16
Mbeki, Thabo 40
miners 7, 27

National Party 12
necklacing 33
Nelson Mandela's Children's Fund 42
Ngoyi, Lilian 15
non-violent protest 11, 14, 19, 39

Pan Africanist Congress (PAC) 18

pass laws 13, 14, 15, 18, 19, 26
police brutality 18, 25, 28, 29, 39

Reconstruction and Development Programme (RDP) 36, 37
Robben Island Prison 20–24, 25, 40

sabotage 19, 20
safe houses 19
Sharpeville massacre 18
Soweto Uprising 24, 25
sports boycotts 30
State of Emergency 28

Tambo, Oliver 14, 24
townships 28, 32, 41
trade unions 26, 27
Treason Trial 16, 17
Truth and Reconciliation Commission (TRC) 38–39
Tutu, Desmond 39

Ubuntu 8, 38, 39
Umkhonto we Sizwe (MK) 19, 20
Union of South Africa 7
United Democratic Front (UDF) 28

voting rights 7, 11, 36

white settlers 4, 7
Witwatersrand University 9
Women's League 15

Youth League 10, 11

Zuma, Jacob 40, 41